Praise for Matt Borczon:

"As a social worker I have a deep interest in Matt Borczon's work. I hope it helped him, and know that it assists others who don't possess his writing skills. From *Saved Rounds* which allowed me to know that social workers and those in the field of psychology have been far too slow to grasp the concept Matt spills out right from the start. In "Afghanistan 2010" we get a glimpse of the stoic mindset of those who serve our country. For, "The Last Poem" Matt rips the curtains back and allows those blinds to snap up to the ceiling, to show everyone how war has affected his beloved wife and family. It was in "Riding An Imaginary Horse", that I received the gut punch or a pretty pink nightmare, compared to the memories and dreams that still sit on that saddle. No one can tell these stories so necessary for understanding our veterans, better than Matt. His gift is the ability to knock us down and drag us through the ravages of war. The poem "The War" made me tear up and then lose my battle on the last stanza. I moved on to "Veterans Day" and had to seriously stop and make myself breathe. This book couldn't stick to the speed limit and never gave you a break as it raced right on through."

-Thasia Ann, author of *Pam's Jacket,* Guerilla Genisis Press

"In *Saved Rounds* Matt Borczon leads us through the nightmare of what is PTSD. This book is full of power packed poems that lets the reader feel the pain and the determination of countless amputees, the screams and cries of the Afghan children and a Navy nurse and his family trying to heal. Do not thank him for his service or for being a hero but instead thank him for these poems, the blood he left on these pages and for being a voice for those who can't."

-Scot Young, author of *Brautigan Meets Bukowski, All Around Cowboy* and publisher at *the Rusty Truck* and *Deuce Coupe*.

More praise for Matt Borczon:

"I've long been envious of the heartbreaking devastation of Matt Borczon's poetry, though perhaps not of the experiences that led him to write it. Matt has complained that many editors don't care for his spare vertical style, but in the case of poems about war, let us remember what outlaw poet Todd Moore said about poems that "hang down the page like long black fuses..." These are poems waiting for you to light them."

-Brian Rihlmann

"This book is a punch to the gut. It hits you where you live. Borczon wastes no words in describing the visible and the unseen scars that war inflicts upon its survivors. The poems are tight, intense snapshots of the poet's experience while serving in Afghanistan. Brutal but not sensationalistic, the power of these poems is undeniable. Once you begin reading, you won't be able to stop. This should be required reading in our turbulent times."

-Kevin M. Hibshman, editor, *FEARLESS* poetry zine

"Matt Borczon's poetry style is as recognizable as Van Gogh's in painting or Davis's in music, here illuminating the human cost behind the grinning deathmask of war with deep insight and unflinching compassion."

-Chuck Joy, poet and child psychiatrist, author: *Said the Growling Dog*, and other poetry collections.

Saved Rounds

Poems by Matt Borczon

Kung Fu Treachery Press
Rancho Cucamonga, CA

Copyright © Matt Borczon, 2021
First Edition: 1 3 5 7 9 10 8 6 4 2
ISBN: 978-1-952411-43-4
LCCN: 2020952982

Cover art: Matt Borczon
Author photo: Matt Borczon
All rights reserved. No part of this publication may be reproduced or transmitted in any form or by any means, electronic or mechanical, including photocopying, recording or by info retrieval system, without prior written permission from the author.

Acknowledgments:

Special thanks to Thasia Ann, Brian Rihlmann and Kevin M.Hibshman, Scot Young

TABLE OF CONTENTS

Saved Rounds / 1

September 2010 / 3

Stuff I Think About / 4

The Last Poem / 6

Amputee # 4 / 7

Amputee #5 / 8

Amputee #6 / 9

Amputee #7 / 10

Amputee #8 / 11

Amputee #9 / 12

Amputee #10 / 13

Recovery / 14

The War / 16

Colin / 17

Someday / 19

Riding an Imaginary Horse / 22

I Cry / 24

Apology / 27

War Machine / 30

Veterans / 32

Riding the Seesaw / 34

Talking / 36

Talking About the Sky / 38

They Say / 40

Dead Bodies # 1 / 42

Dead Bodies # 2 / 44

Dead Bodies # 5 / 46

Parade / 48

A Game We Play / 50

The War / 51

Travel / 54

Disability Rating / 56

Veterans Day / 59

Thanks / 61

A Camp Bastion Reunion / 64

The Trick / 65

How I Knew I Was Mostly Ok / 68

Soft Like the Rain / 69

My Wife/ 73

Inside Joke / 75

Saved Rounds

Saved Rounds

At the
end of
the group
therapy session
the leader
would always
ask for
any saved
rounds which
we thought
was funny
since we
knew he
never served
what he
meant was
were there
any issues
left to
address
any pain
still not
examined
any nightmares
not popped
open like
a can

of tuna
anyone
going home
to beat
their wife
drink too
much or
maybe slit
a wrist
anything
you still
want to
solve in
the remaining
three minutes
most days
no one
says anything
and we
take our
saved rounds
home to
be used
later maybe
on our
families
mostly just
on ourselves.

September 2010

On
the
plane
into
Afghanistan
we
all
pretend
we
are
only
afraid
of
flying.

Stuff I Think About

In Afghanistan
I used
to have
to walk
guard duty
along the
fence and
search the
overflow
tent hospital
all without
a gun
and all
these years
later I
am still
not sure
what bothers
me more
how much
I believed
I needed
that gun
for safety
then
or that
I still

believe
I need
a gun for
safety now
or that
before
the war
I never
thought
I needed
a gun
at all.

The Last Poem

of mine
my wife
read was
about PTSD
and pain
I wrote
about feeling
like I
was drowning
and dragging
her and
the kids
down with
me
she wrapped
her arms
around my
neck and
kissed me
tenderly
on my
head and
said you
always
forget how
well I
swim.

Amputee # 4

Looking at
a Marine
with one
arm gone
and thinking
he was
pretty lucky

was the
day I
realized
I had
been in
Afghanistan
too long.

Amputee #5

Fiercely
Determined
the armless
Marine
swears he
will figure
out how
to hold
his new
daughter.

Amputee # 6

The soldier
asked me
If I knew
what happened
to his
boot

he never
asked
about his
foot.

Amputee #7

the legless
soldier
no longer
tries
to even
remember
the last
time he
wanted
to try.

Amputee #8

In a
VA writing
workshop
the prompt
was the word
Homecoming

with his
remaining
hand the
soldier wrote
I will
let you
know when
I get
there.

Amputee #9

The doctor
says he
is lucky
to live
in these
times

they now
have
wheelchairs
that can
climb stairs.

Amputee # 10

the Amputee
worked hard

in the hospital

determined
to stand
when he
receives his
medal.

Recovery

on many
nights the
ghosts
now leave
me alone

the dead
soldiers
and Marines
are no
longer angry

no longer
screaming into
my dreams

no longer
whispering
into my
ear at
work no
longer telling
me my
wife is

leaving and
my kids
hate me

they are
no longer
convinced
that I
made it
out any
better than
they did

now the
blood on
my hands
is ours

not just
theirs.

The War

is a
stray dog
that I
brought
home one
day and
when it
started to
bite my
children
shit on
my rug
and destroy
my furniture
my wife
complained

I understood
but by
then I
had been
with it
so long
I had
no idea
how to
even try
to make
it leave.

Colin

The crying
soldier said
to his
friend that
Colin was
blown to
pieces
and we
didn't even
stop to
pick them
up
and I
hadn't been
in Afghanistan
long enough
to know
which doctor
was the
Psychiatrist
we were
supposed
to contact
but I
had been
there long
enough to

know telling
him he
did everything
he could
will never
sound like
telling him
he did
enough

Someday

I will
be the
colorful flower
for sale
in the
market
the smile
on my
daughters face
the heart
dotting the
I in
a love
letter

someday I
will be
the wind
against your
neck the
moon's reflection
on the
ocean the
engine of
a leaving
train

someday I
will be
a lion
in the
dead of
winter a
planet in
deep space
a dinosaur
at the
bottom of
the ocean

someday I
will be
a sun
salutation a
Zen koan
a Sumi
painting

someday I
will be
many things
maybe everything

and someday
I will
be something
other than
a memory
of the
war.

Riding an Imaginary Horse

(for Kari Ryan)

In my
darkest nightmare
I watch
my pony
trapped
neck deep
in a
frozen lake
it's slowly
turning blue
and crying
like an
Afghan child
from 2010
while somewhere
a guy
on social
media wants
to know
how I
can be
disabled from
a tour
in a
combat hospital
so I

look everywhere
for a
place to
put down
the saddle
I have
been carrying
in order
to type
an answer
to a
question
I still
don't even
understand

I Cry

at everything
now sad
movies
old songs
the memory
of my
father and
friends gone
too soon
it makes
me uneasy
and I
try to
hide it
from my
wife and
children who
always notice
but never
ask me
about it
I am
not ashamed
or confused
by it and
I am
reminded nightly

in flashbacks
and nightmares
that in
Afghanistan
I felt
completely numb
after all
those soldiers
civilians and
children shot
dismembered
or killed
I remember
the amount
of blood
and the
smell of
bleach used
to clean
the beds
after we
removed the
bodies
I remember
an officer
telling us
about compassion
fatigue
I remember
thinking my

feelings were
just another
thing I
lost in
the war.

Apology

I used
to keep
a diary
when I
was in
Afghanistan
I thought
it would
explain to
my family
what was
wrong with
me then
and now
but it
was only
filled with
cause and
effect IED
and amputation
gun shots
and wound-vacs
helicopters and
blood
it never
came close
to explaining

how I
can want
both to
protect you
from all
of it and
how bad
I want
you all to
understand
my fear
my nightmares
my panic
in crowded
rooms the
blood I
still see
on my
clothes the
nights I
can't sleep
and all
the time
I spend
apologizing
to you
for trying
to make
you my
therapist for

trying to
make you
understand
that the
only house
I wanted
to burn
to the
ground was
my own

War Machine

I have
held your
secrets
like the
skin of
a snake
and swallowed
my country's
sword to
the hilt
as I
doused myself
in kerosene
and set
fire to
my clothes
turning the
sky the
color of
an exploding
desert sun
my screams
sound like
Afghanistan
in 2010
as my
skin turned

to ash
and sand
disappearing
on an
angry wind
as white
eyebrow generals
figure out
how to
do it
all again.

Veterans

On Memorial
day someone
always thinks
it is appropriate
to thank
me for
my service
and I
have to
fight back
the urge
to scream
at them
that Memorial
day is really
about the
service men
and women
who died
serving their
country
not me
I am
in fact
alive and
I am
told by

my psychiatrist
that if
I take
my medication
and keep
saying this
over and
over

that
some day
I might
believe it.

Riding the Seesaw

My youngest
gets thrown
forward
cutting her
chin deep
as she
falls off
and she
cries while
blood covers
her hand
and then
runs down
her arm

and I
hate myself
in this
moment

for finding
myself back
in Afghanistan
in Bastion
Hospital
a thousand
miles from

my daughter
and still
a million
miles from
home.

Talking

To the
VA Psychiatrist
I tell
him about
the total
flashback
I had
when my
daughter
fell off
the see- saw
crying with
blood running
down her
arms as
she held
her chin

he says
it is
important
not to
feel defeated
when I
experience
a setback
and that

there is
only so
much better
you ever
get with
PTSD

and I
am surprised
that he
thinks
I feel
victory or
defeat

I am
surprised
he thinks
I feel
anything
at all.

Talking About the Sky

They say
heaven is
on its
other side
and maybe
it goes
on forever
and I
saw a
movie once
where a
Viet Nam
vet tried
to shoot
the stars
out with
a machine
gun and
a red
moon means
something
to sailors
but I
can't remember
what and
Afghanistan
was a

whole different
place when
the sun
went down
and everything
got quiet

it felt
like every
star was
pointing
toward home
back when I
still thought
I knew
where that
was

and
that I
would get
there eventually.

They Say

The sunset
over Presque Isle
is the
third most
beautiful
in the
whole world
and I
never wanted
to travel
any farther
from home
then maybe
North East Pa
just wanted
to walk
the Erie
streets
wearing old
sneakers maybe
raise a
family but
only on
the west
side I
really only
ever wanted
to be
home

17 years
later and
7 countries
beside Afghanistan
2,268 coalition
and local
national troops
thousands of
nightmares
3 jobs
2 medications
3 different
therapists and
one support
group and
that beautiful
sunset no
longer feels
like mine

and home
just feels
like
another thing
I lost
in the
war.

Dead Bodies # 1

The
soldier
in
the
ER
in
Helmand
didn't
have
enough
of
a
face
to
be
alive
so
I
was
Surprised
that
he
was

and
not
surprised

later
when
he
wasn't
anymore.

Dead Bodies # 2

The
child
in
the
isolation
room
looked
calm
asleep
even
which
was
alarming
considering
how
many
nurses
were
standing
there
crying
loud
and
out
of
control
finally

Brian
decided
to
carry
the
dead
child's
body
to
the
morgue

he
could
tell
nobody
else
wanted
to
and
he
was
getting
tired
of
the
noise.

Dead Bodies # 5

They
took
the
body
of
the
Taliban
Leader
away
but
listening
to
the
cries
of
his
5
Year
old
daughter
felt
worse
than
trying
to

close
his
eyes
with
my
thumbs.

Parade

In Afghanistan
when a
British soldier
died they
had a
ceremony
and the
hospital would
stop for
a short
while as
they loaded
the coffin
to send
it home
they called
this a
parade

one day
Phil asks
why I
never go
to the
parade and
I mutter
under my

breath something
about hating
marching bands
and clown
with big feet

and how
war and
parades are
only ever
funny in
that way
that only
makes you
want to
cry.

A Game We Play

The VA
psychiatrist
says there
are medications
that would
make me
feel better
and wonders
out loud
why I
would not
want to
FEEL BETTER
and I
reply for
like maybe
the 15th
time that
before we
work on
feeling better
shouldn't we
figure out
why I
can't feel
anything
at all.

The War

makes me
shake like
leaves in
hurricane
winds makes
me roar
like a
lion lie
like the
devil and
pray like
a saint

the war
makes me
walk like
a zombie
cry like
a baby
sleep like
I'm dead

It's a
pill I
swallow and
a noose
I stick

my head
through

the war
is a
child I
carry dead
wrapped in
a blue
towel
it is
a wound
vac I
wipe clean
daily a
bed I
spray with
bleach and
a uniform
I can't
get the
blood out
of

the war
is a
flag I
fold in
the shape
of a

triangle
every day

to give
to the
grieving wife
and family
of the
man I
have become.

Travel

In fifth
grade we
went to
Canada
to visit
the falls
and the
wax museum
and I
remember
being scared
as the
bus crossed
this huge
bridge afraid
we would
fall into
the water
and I
think I
decided then
I didn't
want to
travel anywhere
ever again
and 35
years later

flying into
Afghanistan
shoulder to
shoulder with
150 Navy
sailors praying
we didn't get
shot out
of the
sky I
knew I
was right.

Disability Rating

Never tell
anyone
that you
are both
disabled
and cleared
to work
never tell
them that
you get
the money
tax free
and you
will get
it for
the rest
of your
life
because
someone
always says
something like
it must
be nice
or they
should be
so lucky

and I
never know
how to
tell them
that this
is the
price of
my screaming
nightmares
my sleepless
nights and
the anxious
face I
make in
crowds this
is the
price of
depressed
Saturday mornings
and the
price of
my kids
not knowing
how to
talk to
me anymore
and I
never even
try to
explain that

I would
give it
all back
with interest
if my
wife could
feel safe
enough to
not sleep
so far
on the
other side
of our
bed.

Veterans Day

My 11
year old
daughter
says dad
we studied
veterans day
in school
today you
are a
veteran right
yes honey
I say
my teacher
says you
fought for
our freedom
my teacher
says you
defended our
country my
teacher says
you are
a hero
I ask
her what
do you
think about
all that

and she
asks me
how old
she was
when I
was in
Afghanistan
when I
tell her
she was
only two
years old
she says
I mostly
just remember
how much
I missed you

and I
hug her
too long
and too
tight as
I say
all these
years later
that is
what I
most remember
too.

Thanks

A friend
said to
me that
at least
you have
a kind
of trauma
they thank
you for
that survivors
of sexual
assault or
incest are
paranoid
and always
angry in
a world
that doesn't
want to
hear about
it that
wants them
to suffer
in silence
that no
one thanks
them for

their survival
like they
thank a
vet for
their service
and I
know she
is right
I know
people
are quicker
to understand
that PTSD
is not
something
I control
quicker to
forgive my
anger or
anxiety and
all the
awful things
I sometimes
do
but honestly
some days
thank you
for your
service just
sounds like

thank you
for screaming
at your
children
thank you
for day
drinking
all weekend
thank you
for avoiding
your own
mother
thanks for
the therapy
you skip
the job
you no
longer
care about
and thank
you for
all the
nights your
ghosts still
rub up
against you
then warn
you not
to tell.

A Camp Bastion Reunion

Just shouldn't
happen
because if
you put
Kari Brian
and me
in the
same room

the ghost
of that
afghan child
will be
so real

everyone
will hear
it's last
breath.

The Trick

I
have
too
normal
a
life
for
the
things
I've
seen
4
kids
a
marriage
that
works
a
job
overtime
vacation
time
a
cottage
on
the
lake

for
3
weeks
a
year
but
that
is
the
trick
though
isn't
it

success
is
taking
all
the
shit
the
war
shipped
me
home
with
all
the
missing
limbs

under
surgical
light
all
the
thudding
echoes
of
coffin
lids
closing
forever

and
keeping
all
of
it
behind
my
eyes.

How I Knew I Was Mostly Ok

Was because
I didn't
have a
specific
plan to
kill myself
my fantasy
wasn't about
blood it
was just
the moment
when the
helicopter blades
stopped turning
the wound
vacs stopped
humming the
children stopped
crying
it was
like the
moment
all the
birds
stop chirping
just before
the hurricane
begins.

Soft Like the Rain

This morning
under dark
skies I
feel myself
fall backwards
into that
hot sweaty
place
I try
to hide
the war
in
lately it's
the sound
of children
crying like
crows in
a graveyard
it leaves
me doubting
things I
know and
lived through
was it
really just
one Afghan
child or

did we kill
more was
Brian's story
about picking
it up when
no one
else wanted
to the
same child
I took
care of
for days
and was
it the same
baby they
injected with
enough pain
meds to
kill a
water buffalo
when they
decided they
could not
save it
is it
or
is it
all different
children I
no longer

trust myself
to remember
I have
carried so
many dead
children in
dreams these
last nine
years and
Brian and
I never
compared notes
and we almost
never talk
at all now
so I
don't know
what his
ghosts
look like
and I
don't think
about it
unless
I have
to but
I have
to like
death and
taxes or

sunrise and
the lunar
tide all
those things
that just
happen and
we brought
all those
kids back
with us
like dog
tags and
foot lockers
you pack
into the
back of
your basement
but some
nights I
still hear
them crying
soft like
the rain.

My Wife

asks me
to take
our daughter
to Wednesday
morning mass
I laugh
and tell
my daughter
not to
stand too
close in
case God
is mad
because I
never went
to church
on deployment
my youngest
says but
daddy you
did pray
didn't you
and I
don't know
how to
tell her
I only

prayed
when somebody
died
so instead
I just
tell her
that I
prayed almost
every day.

Inside Joke

I rolled
into work
at seven
and told
my boss
I had
already taken
my client
to the
hospital for
his scheduled
surgery then
I picked
up discharge
papers on
another guy
scanned them
and set
up his
follow up
appointment
my boss
shakes his
head and
asks how
I get
so much
done so
early

it's easy
if you
don't sleep
I say
and he
says I
wish you
could tell
me how
to do
that and
I try
to imagine
telling him
it's simple
go to
war for
10 months
learn to
jump at
every sound
worry the
base will
be shelled
or you
will be
shot listen
always for
helecopters
That will
mean it's
time to

run to
your work
station in
the hospital
hand a
dead infant
back to
it's mother
and spend
10 years
trying to
forget the
look in
that mother's
eyes
but I
don't say
that instead
I say
Tom if
I told
you I
might have
to kill
you
I listen
to him
chuckle
as I
walk away.
I

Matthew Borczon is a poet and writer from Erie, Pa. He has published ten books of poetry the most recent being *Ghost Highway Blues* through Alien Buddha press. He has been nominated for a pushcart and a best of the Net. He works as both a US Navy sailor and as a nurse for adults with developmental disabilities. He has a wife and four kids and not enough time to write.